# The Election of 1828: The History of the Race Between Andrew Jackson and John Quincy Adams that Ended the Era of Good Feelings

## By Charles River Editors

Andrew Jackson

## About Charles River Editors

**Charles River Editors** provides superior editing and original writing services across the digital publishing industry, with the expertise to create digital content for publishers across a vast range of subject matter. In addition to providing original digital content for third party publishers, we also republish civilization's greatest literary works, bringing them to new generations of readers via ebooks.

Sign up here to receive updates about free books as we publish them, and visit Our Kindle Author Page to browse today's free promotions and our most recently published Kindle titles.

# Introduction

**John Quincy Adams**

## The Election of 1828

"'Ought a convicted adulteress and her paramour husband to be placed in the highest offices of this free and Christian land?'" – Excerpt from a newspaper article attacking Andrew Jackson and his wife in 1828

George Washington, the first President of the United States, warned against the formation of political parties, but it did not take long for American politicians to ignore him and draw a line in the sand regarding the power of the federal government and that of the individual states. That said, the line ebbed away among the bloodshed of the War of 1812, and until the election of 1828, American politics experienced the so-called Era of Good Feelings, during which Americans took heed of Washington's words and set aside party lines for a supposed new era of political cooperation.

Following the tradition begun by his predecessors, James Monroe refused to run for a third term in office in 1824, leaving the White House wide open in the most regionally divisive election in American history. It began with John Quincy Adams, who was the favored candidate of the New England states. They recognized and respected his lifelong service to his country, as well as his experience and intellect. On the other hand, Southern voters favored Henry Clay, the acclaimed Speaker of the House who helped broker the Missouri Compromise, and they believed "The Great Compromiser" had the skills needed to continue to navigate the increasingly turbulent waters surrounding slavery. Meanwhile, William Crawford had the support of former presidents Jefferson and Madison but was in very poor health. Finally, Andrew Jackson had made quite a name for himself in the famous Battle of New Orleans and was the darling of the rugged people settling the expanding American West. All of the candidates were members of the Democratic-Republican Party, though Adams appealed to the former Federalists in New England thanks to his famous father.

**Clay**

Not surprisingly, when Election Day rolled around, no candidate gained a majority in the Electoral College. While Jackson had won a plurality of the popular vote and electoral votes, he did not have the necessary majority of electoral votes needed to secure the presidency. In keeping with the rules laid down by the 12th Amendment, the House of Representatives had to choose between the top three candidates: Jackson, Adams and Crawford. Clay came in fourth and would never be president. However, he remained Speaker of the House and thus had tremendous influence over who would.

While Clay disagreed vehemently with Adams over the issue of slavery, the two men agreed on most other matters, including higher tariffs and the need for internal improvements in America's roads and waterways. Thus, he threw his support behind Adams, who was chosen president by the House with the first ballot, cast on February 9, 1825.

Having won the most votes, Jackson was already upset that he was not given the presidency, but when John Quincy Adams appointed Henry Clay to be his Secretary of State after Clay had played kingmaker in the House and thrown his support behind Adams, the Jacksonian Democrats were enraged. With accusations that the two had reached a corrupt bargain behind closed doors, Adams was already tainted before he could even start governing the nation. To understand the context of Jackson's accusations, it's necessary to remember that during this era, the office of Secretary of State, not Vice President, was seen as the conduit to the presidency.

Adams had been in politics for most of his adult life, but his contemporaries and historians were both puzzled by the fact that he either refused to play politics or did not know how. Some have speculated that he did not like being president, while others have pointed to the Jacksonians also refusing to play ball due to their displeasure with the election results. It has even been speculated that Adams suffered from depression, which also made him a more private man. Whatever the case, Adams would not spend his time in office trying to develop political support for his positions.

While Adams was a statesman, indeed the last of the first generation of American statesmen, he was no politician. He served not because he loved power or prestige, but because he felt it was his duty. Like his five predecessors, he felt it was beneath his dignity to campaign for any office. However, the times were changing, and his supporters had no such qualms, nor did those supporting Jackson. Thus, after a campaign characterized by vile mud-slinging and personal attacks, Jackson defeated Adams in 1828.

Jackson's presidential bid in 1828 a new era dawned in American politics: the birth of the two party system. Jackson and Adams had both been Democratic-Republicans, the Jeffersonian Party, but their election had helped split up that original party, and thus Jackson's election marked the true beginning of the country's current Democratic Party. Furthermore, in many ways, the election of 1828 bore the hallmarks of the first modern election. Like his father a generation earlier, Adams left the presidency a bitter man, refusing even to attend Jackson's inauguration, but he made clear to his friends that he would like to be elected to the U.S. House of Representatives. His supporters rallied around him, and in 1830 he returned to Washington as a Congressman, becoming the first president to remain in politics after leaving the White House.

*The Election of 1828: The History of the Race Between Andrew Jackson and John Quincy Adams that Ended the Era of Good Feelings* chronicles one of America's most important campaigns. Along with pictures of people, places, and events, you will learn about the Election of 1828 like never before.

## The Era of Good Feelings

Like the previous election, the cast of characters for the 1828 presidential election included an eclectic bunch that demonstrated the growing rifts in the nation's ideologies as it sectionalized and struggled to define itself and its political structure.

As Andrew Jackson's star rose, he would come to showcase this rift all too clearly. Born in the Waxhaws of South Carolina before the American Revolution, Jackson hailed from Scotch-Irish stock near the border with North Carolina, the mountainous realm far removed from the plantations further south. When war reached the future state in 1780, Jackson quickly gained a burning hatred for the British when an officer struck Jackson across the face with his sword after the young boy refused to clean the officer's boots.[i] Following the war, the young Jackson joined hands with a rough group of frontier youths, spending his days drinking, gambling, and racking up debts. To pay those debts Jackson bet his last possession, a horse, on a dice game, won, and left the Waxhaws for good.[ii]

Though Jackson's mother hoped he would enter the ministry, the cantankerous, rough-hewn youth instead entered law. Lacking any real formal education at the present age of seventeen, Jackson nonetheless convinced an attorney in Salisbury, North Carolina, to take him on as an apprentice, law schools being thin on the ground at the time.[iii] Supposedly "...the most roaring, rollicking, game-cocking, horse-racing, card-playing, mischievous fellow that ever lived in Salisbury" according to one resident, Jackson would study by day and spend the night drinking, gambling, and relocating outhouses.[iv]

In 1787, the 20 year old Jackson presented himself for the period's equivalent of the bar exam. Obtaining his state law license, Jackson set up his shingle in Guilford County.[v] His law career floundering, he received word from a friend from Salisbury who'd become a superior court judge in the Western District of North Carolina, later to be known as Tennessee.[vi] Offered the position of district public prosecutor, Jackson went west to forge a new life for himself, as many did before and after. With a few friends Jackson set up shop in Jonesborough, setting the stage for his future association with the West.[vii]

Eventually he moved further west to the new town of Nashville, which then had a population of roughly 200. Marriage to a not yet quite divorced Rachel Donelson occurred around this time as well, though the fully legal marriage would not occur until 1794.[viii]

That same year, Jackson was appointed attorney general for the Mero District of the Tennessee Territory. He also entered politics and the military, engaging in land speculation and serving in the local militia.[ix] These beginnings quickly became a full-fledged political career, as Jackson not only participated in the 1796 convention to draft a state constitution, but was also elected Tennessee's first Congressman.[x]

Jackson was rough-hewn, temperamental, and above all, Western (by the standards of the time), whereas his counterpart for the 1828 election was almost a perfect embodiment of everything Jackson was not and would come to oppose and despise.

Born the same year as Jackson in Braintree, Massachusetts, Adams played a large role in setting the stage for the election in 1828.[xi] Descended from Puritan stock, the environment that John Quincy Adams grew up in contrasted almost perfectly with Jackson's – while Jackson was on the frontier, Adams lived among packed New England towns filled with stuffy Yankee faith and money. While the South contained strong Tory leanings, New England epitomized the Revolutionary cause, its interests a major impetus for the war overall.

As Jackson entered Congress for the first time, John Quincy Adams' father, John Adams, became the second President of the United States in its first contested election in 1796. The Federalist faction triumphed over the Republican faction, though the two groups were too dissociated and regional to truly be called parties at the time.[xii] The Federalists, a largely New England group, stated they represented the Constitution and its ideals. The Republicans countered by stating their cause was against the New England oligarchy.[xiii]

This early election spawned many ideas on republicanism, including the nature of a republican government, and even political parties. For the Republicans, the power of an oligarchy threatened the liberty of the people, and with George Washington still fresh in their minds, the idea of political parties rubbed them the wrong way. John Adams himself wrote of his fears of a two-party system rending the nation apart.[xiv]

His son, meanwhile, after graduating from Harvard University in 1787, studied law and entered the bar in 1790. While Jackson thrived in law, either in spite of or because of his personality, Adams disliked practicing law, and he spent his early career writing political editorials, mostly in defense of the Washington administration and lambasting Thomas Paine for his unreserved support of the French Revolution.[xv]

As the 18th century ended and the 19th century dawned, Adams did his best to avoid the increased factionalism affecting not only American politics but the burgeoning factions themselves.[xvi] His rejection of politics did not last, and in 1802 Adams reluctantly joined the ranks of the bloodied Federalists to become a Massachusetts State Senator. The next year, Adams became a U.S. Senator.[xvii]

The Adams political legacy did not quite haunt young John Quincy - he was expected to enter politics and to sign on with the party of his father, but those ideas lined up with his for the most part anyway.[xviii] Tied to the region and its interests, the reluctant Adams watched as foreign problems boiled over to engulf the nation in the first war of its young life.

The War of 1812 proved to be a turning point in American politics, as most wars do. First and foremost, it destroyed the Federalists as a political faction; their musings to secede from the nation prior to war's end reeked of sedition.[xix] It also launched Jackson's name onto the national stage as the hero of the hour, the victor of New Orleans in a battle stunning for its lopsidedness.[xx]

The presidential election of 1816 reflected the Federalists' crumbling state in the wake of the War of 1812's conclusion. The Republican candidate, James Monroe, secured 183 of the available 217 electoral votes, while Federalist Rufus King managed a mere 34.[xxi] The state votes for King came, unsurprisingly, from the New England states of Maine, Massachusetts, and Connecticut, but even his home state of New York swung to Monroe. The future border state of Delaware with its meager three delegates also supported King.[xxii]

**Monroe**

Monroe looked to the bright side of the end of the two-party system, stating in his inaugural address that the American people were "one great family with a common interest" and that the sort of conflict brought by factions and parties "does not belong to our system."[xxiii] Taking Washington's words to heart, the ideology of the Era of Good Feelings came to the forefront of American politics.

Jackson and Adams, meanwhile, entered new stages in their political careers. Jackson, the hero of New Orleans, took full advantage of his fame as he undertook a triumphal tour that ended in Washington, D.C.[xxiv] Adams, meanwhile, having served in Ghent to help end the war, found himself appointed Secretary of State under the Monroe administration, a choice lauded by Jackson as "the best selection, to fill the Department of State…"[xxv]

Jackson and Adams represented a new generation of political leaders, ones who grew up in the wake of the Revolution but were too young to actively participate in the Revolution itself. The Monroe administration represented the older generation; the first transition of generational politics in the nation's history.[xxvi] With both Jackson and Adams turning 50 in 1817, the young Republic looked away from the entanglements of European politics towards the American frontiers. As the Transportation Revolution began with the start of the Erie Canal, the post-war political landscape Jackson and Adams entered turned very different from the political world they first entered.[xxvii]

One of the new issues the second generation faced put them in conflict with the still influential first generation of American politicians. With the birth of a new Republic rose the clamor for the people's voice to reach their government, something Americans felt denied them under the British Crown and a major impetus for the Revolution in the first place.[xxviii] The older generation, with thoughts of Philosopher Kings and a belief that only those "with a stake in society" need bother with politics, disagreed with the idea of a more democratic republic.[xxix]

With many states either lifting or entering the Union without property requirements for voters, the resultant political shifts changed the politics in the nation forever, bringing a more open government, an ideology in conflict with the more distant government extolled by the first generation.[xxx] With a widening vote, the one-party state of the nation found itself less united, and despite Monroe's easy reelection in 1820, the party itself was, in the words of Adams, "assuming daily more a character of cabal…"[xxxi]

### Prelude to the Election of 1824

Before the election of 1820, which helped put Adams on the national stage, the First Seminole War enhanced Jackson's prestige, added Florida to the nation, and nearly started a war with Spain and Great Britain. In 1817, hostilities with the natives boiled over into open warfare, with the locals allying with escaped slaves to attack the U.S. Army and the Army responding in kind. When the Army attacked a native town on the Georgia side of the border, the natives and their allies responded by attacking a boat loaded with American soldiers and their dependents on the Florida side, beginning the First Seminole War in earnest.[xxxii]

Secretary of War John C. Calhoun issued orders to the general in the region, Edmund Gaines, to demand reparations from the Seminoles. If reparations did not come, General Gaines was authorized to march into Florida and subdue them. He was, however, prohibited from attacking the Spanish, America's disgruntled former ally during the Revolution, even if they were harboring Seminoles.[xxxiii]

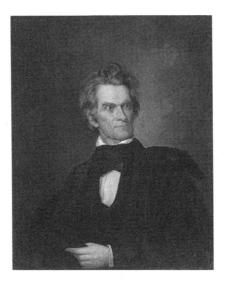

**Calhoun**

**Gaines**

Despite General Gaines' early success in securing a well-known smuggling hub, Calhoun transferred command of the theater to General Jackson, in a desire for a more energetic, aggressive commander with a knowledge and understanding of native warfare (Jackson had fought the Creeks in 1813).[xxxiv] General Jackson already had a reputation for disobeying orders and a disregard of civilian oversight of the military that frightened the government, so he received strict orders not to attack the Spanish.[xxxv]

Jackson, naturally, proceeded to ignore these orders and conquer Spanish Florida for the United States. In a letter to Monroe loaded with plausible deniability, Jackson declared, "Let it be signified to me through any channel that the possession of the Floridas would be desirable to the United States, and in sixty days it will be accomplished."[xxxvi] With a regiment of Tennessee militiamen and backroom discussions with Tennessee Congressman John Rhea to avoid any possible implications of Monroe directly, General Jackson proceeded to conquer Florida, wiping away the scattered remains of the Spanish Empire in the territory.[xxxvii]

Ultimately, it took Jackson three months, not two, but he did stop along the way to hang people, specifically two subjects of Great Britain accused by the American government of arming and instigating the Seminoles, and two Seminole chiefs as well. Though the two whites received a sham trial of sorts before their sentence, the two natives did not.[xxxviii]

While Jackson proceeded to start two international incidents and incite the natives, Adams negotiated with Spain for the purchase of Florida. The proud Spanish Empire proved reluctant to cede the territory prior to Jackson's invasion. As added embarrassment to the government, Monroe himself learned of the executions through newspapers, as Jackson's dispatches took their time arriving in a pre-telegraph strewn America.[xxxix]

Madrid, London, and Washington all called for blood, and the Monroe administration took its time responding. No less a man than the great orator Henry Clay condemned the general's actions, reminding the American people of hostile Europeans' constant accusations that the Americans had "an inordinate spirit of aggrandizement –of coveting other people's goods."[xl] He warned about giving "a fatal sanction, in this infant period of our republic, scarcely two score years old, to military insubordination."[xli] To not condemn Jackson would be "a triumph of the principle of insubordination –a triumph of the military over the civil authority- a triumph over the powers of this house –a triumph over the constitution of the land."[xlii]

Adams, meanwhile, took advantage of Jackson's efforts to adopt a hard line against Spain. With their defenses shattered and strength weakened by colonial revolutions and the Peninsular Campaigns of Napoleon, Adams believed Jackson's efforts presented the best chance for the nation to obtain Florida.[xliii] Adams' words to Spain were used by Jackson's supporters to laud his actions and dismiss the accusations put forth by Clay. To Spain, Adams declared that Jackson's invasion was justified by "the supreme law of nature and nations, the law of self-defense… to enter Spanish territory of Florida in pursuit of, and to destroy, hostile, murdering savages, not bound by obligation, who were without the practice of any moral principle reciprocally obligatory on nations."[xliv]

Clay, as many politicians did at the time, underestimated Jackson's appeal to the people of America who approved of his actions and propelled his career even further. Appealing directly to the people was a new concept in America, and Jackson was one of the first to take advantage of the increasing democratization of the nation.[xlv] Despite his defense of the man and efforts to secure Florida for the nation – a *fait accompli* sans the technical matter of paperwork - the New Englander looked at Jackson's enhanced success with wariness. Writing in his diary, Adams noted regarding the general's visit to the White House, "From the earnestness with which the company pressed round him, and the eye of respect and gratitude which from every quarter beamed upon him, it has as much appearance of being his drawing-room as the President's."[xlvi]

Shortly after that entry, the two visited each other's homes for dinner, a classic case of two politicians playing politics. Already wise to the game, Jackson toured the Northern cities to bask in his fame, though a Senate condemnation forced him to return to Washington to prepare a defense for himself.[xlvii] The Senate condemned the executions of the two British men as "an unnecessary act of severity on the part of a commanding general and a departure from that mild and humane system… honorable to the national character."[xlviii] Fortunately for Jackson, the resolution's approval came shortly before Congress's adjournment. The matter was tabled and quickly faded into obscurity.[xlix]

While Jackson basked in the people's adoration and political impotence, Adams fought to formally secure Florida. Though most of the Spanish forts once again flew the Spanish Empire's flag, several areas remained under American occupation.[l] Adams, as previously noted, took a hard line against Spain, an aging empire recovering from the Napoleonic Wars and struggling and failing to reclaim its New World holdings in South America, which had taken advantage of Spain's occupation by French forces to declare independence.[li]

Adams, smelling blood, strove to acquire Florida, and, if possible, secure Spain's acknowledgement of the Louisiana Purchase, a lingering sore point between the two nations.[lii] Moreover, Adams desired a definite boundary between Spanish California and the Oregon Territory, a place held and occupied by the Americans, British, and (in theory) Russians. Through Oregon the government hoped to break into the lucrative Chinese trade and secure a shorter route than having to circumvent South America.[liii] Adams pushed to make sure Americans obtained the west banks of the rivers to secure American commercial interests in the region, a point that had led to the Louisiana Purchase itself.[liv] The Adams-Onis Treaty also solidified the borders of New Spain, as part of the affirmation of the boundaries of the Louisiana Purchase.[lv]

Less than four months later, Mexico gained independence, nullifying the treaty and necessitating another diplomatic effort by Adams and creating a new headache for the American government. Before the aftermath of the fall of Spain's New World Empire, Adams also dealt with another sticking point in American foreign policy: Oregon. The Oregon Country, a vast, sprawling land of trees and rain, quickly earned a reputation amongst the fur trade for its rich lands. British, American, and Russian eyes looked longingly on the region. Carefully negotiating with the British while endeavoring to avoid looking pro-British to the Crown's detractors in the government, Adams' efforts regarding Oregon concluded with the Treaty of 1818, an agreement between the United States and Great Britain that settled the borders of the Oregon Country and excluded the tenuous Russian interests in the region.[lvi]

Adams' efforts succeeded. The Adams-Onis Treaty of 1819 secured Florida for the United

States at the cost of five million dollars. The treaty solidified the boundaries of the Louisiana Purchase, stating, "The Boundary Line between the two Countries, West of the Mississippi, shall begin on the Gulf of Mexico, at the mouth of the River Sabine in the Sea, continuing North, along the Western Bank of that River, to the 32d degree of Latitude; thence by a Line due North to the degree of Latitude, where it strikes the Rio Roxo of Natchitoches, or Red River, then following the course of the Rio-Roxo Westward to the degree of Longitude, 100 West from London and 23 from Washington, then crossing the said Red River, and running thence by a Line due North to the River Arkansas, thence, following the Course of the Southern bank of the Arkansas to its source in Latitude, 42. North and thence by that parallel of Latitude to the South-Sea."[lvii]

Despite the settling of borders between Spain (and later Mexico) and Great Britain, Adams soon found a new international threat in Czar Alexander I and his Holy Alliance. In 1821, the czar issued an official edict warning foreign ships not to enter within a hundred miles of Russian Alaska, a lonely land barely occupied by a handful of miserable traders subsidized by the Russian government.[lviii] Adams took a hard line with Russia just as he did with Spain, and Russia backed down from its Alaska policy due to British interests in the region. Thus, Adams not only cowed the European power of Spain, he also successfully negotiated favorable deals with one of the emerging European powers and continued the détente between the Republic and the British Crown.

**Czar Alexander I**

As Secretary of State, Adams fashioned the Monroe Doctrine of 1823; the declaration of the Monroe administration that European nations had no business meddling in the New World, and that the United States would protect the infant republics birthed from Spain's aging empire.[lix] Receiving envoys from the new nations forged in the fires of Spain's revolutions, the Monroe Doctrine in several ways attacked the Holy Alliance of Russia, Prussia, and Austria. and their interests in reconquering the New World. With Great Britain's full support thanks to their economic interests with the new republics, the Doctrine declared, "At the proposal of the Russian Imperial Government, made through the minister of the Emperor residing here, a full power and instructions have been transmitted to the minister of the United States at St. Petersburg to arrange by amicable negotiation the respective rights and interests of the two nations on the northwest coast of this continent. A similar proposal had been made by His Imperial Majesty to the Government of Great Britain, which has likewise been acceded to. The Government of the United States has been desirous by this friendly proceeding of manifesting the great value which they have invariably attached to the friendship of the Emperor and their solicitude to cultivate the best understanding with his Government. In the discussions to which this interest has given rise and in the arrangements by which they may terminate the occasion has been judged proper for asserting, as a principle in which the rights and interests of the United States are involved, that the American continents, by the free and independent condition which they have assumed and maintain, are henceforth not to be considered as subjects for future colonization by any European powers.".[lx] The Doctrine went on to add, "We owe it, therefore, to candor and to the amicable relations existing between the United States and those powers to declare that we should consider any attempt on their part to extend their system to any portion of this hemisphere as dangerous to our peace and safety."[lxi]

Though many European governments despised the Doctrine, it would form the backbone of American foreign policy in the New World for the next century. It was also largely the creation of Adams, despite its name.

Through these international victories, Adams found an unlikely ally of sorts in the man who'd caused one of the great debacles of the Monroe administration: Andrew Jackson. Despite the massive headache Jackson's efforts in Florida caused, he did succeed, with all the subtlety and diplomatic nuance he possessed, to obtain Florida for the U.S., checking off a diplomatic goal the young nation harbored more or less since its inception. Adams looked on Jackson as a man who did things. Jackson, in turn, recognized the stuffy Yankee's obvious talent, remarking to a friend, "You know my private opinion of Mr. Adams' Talents, virtue, and integrity, and I am free to declare that I have never changed this opinion of Mr. Adams since it was first formed, I think him a man of first rate mind of any in America as a civilian and scholar, and I have never doubted of his attachment to our republican Government."[lxii] Adams, in turn, wrote in his diary, "General Jackson has rendered such services to this Nation, that it is impossible for me to contemplate his character or conduct without reservation."[lxiii]

### 1824

As Monroe's second term concluded, the president maintained his belief that parties were a curse upon the nation. However, the Era of Good Feelings were not as good as some hoped, for political fighting remained, with New England's burgeoning industry and commerce a stark contrast to the rest of the nation. Furthermore, with the nation expanding westward, a new factor entered American politics as territories gained statehood.[lxiv] In the wake of these changes, the nation faced new problems, problems that further divided the supposedly factionless government.

The first economic panic struck the nation in the wake of the War of 1812. The rise of banks and the creation of the Second Bank of the United States rose as a prominent issue following the war. A group of politicians, led by Clay and Calhoun, also took issue with constitutional interpretation.[lxv]

A further issue lay in the need for American infrastructure; the Clay-Calhoun faction believed the poor state of America's roads and canals required federal support to bolster them. Both men looked at these issues from a war hawk perspective – the nation needed a strong economy to fund war, a stringent interpretation of the constitution to preserve the people's rights against wartime dictatorship, and roads and canals to move troops and supplies quickly and efficiently.[lxvi] Adams, unsurprisingly, supported the bank and the interests it represented. Though Jackson would become the bank's greatest enemy, early on he lacked an official opinion, busy as he was fighting duels, conquering territories, and defending himself from Congressional accusations for the previously mentioned duels and conquests.[lxvii]

Yet another issue would prove a sticking point in American politics, one that would not be settled until the Civil War soaked most of the states in blood. Slavery, the elephant of the room in American politics until Reconstruction and even overshadowing the ever-important tariff debates, proved another divisive issue in the burgeoning nation. Jackson, a Southern landowner if not a gentleman, owned slaves and considered slavery the natural place for blacks.[lxviii] As with so many things in his life, Jackson took the slavery issue personally, stating once to his nephew, "They [the 'Eastern interests' as he called them] will find the southern and western states equally resolved to support their constitutional rights."[lxix]

Meanwhile, Adams, the quintessential New England gentleman, modified his views as economics and morality required. Early in his career he condemned slavery morally but admitted its economic uses as understood by economic knowledge of the time.[lxx] By the 1820s, however, his position altered with the times, privately writing that slavery was "the great and foul stain upon the North American Union."[lxxi] Adams also looked disdainfully on the Southern gentlemen: "With the Declaration of Independence on their lips, and the merciless scourge of slavery in their hands, a more flagrant image of human inconsistency can scarcely be conceived than one of our Southern slave-holding republicans."[lxxii]

Adams saw slavery as a dividing line between North and South, as it indeed came to be. Jackson, in turn, saw the issue as one between the West and the South against "Eastern interests." The first true politician from the West, Jackson never clicked with the urban elite of Eastern politics, whose interests he saw as starkly different from those of the South and West. Their seeming indifference to the Southern needs for low tariffs and the Westerner's needs for Indian lands rankled him, and he, like many from his home regions, considered the Easterners little better than the British Jackson so detested.[lxxiii]

As these issues came to the forefront of American politics, creating factions and undermining the so-called Era of Good Feelings, the factions, still too fractured and unorganized to call parties, started preparing for the Election of 1824. Part of this preparation included Adams' detractors making their opinions known. The exceptional successes of the man did not make him immune to politics any more than it did Jackson. The difference, of course, was Jackson cared little for the opinions of other politicians as long as the people supported him. Adams, firmly entrenched in the political machine and circles of Washington and New England, with the Federalist legacy of his father always behind him, lacked such an escape.

Clay criticized Adams as well as Jackson, condemning Adams and the Monroe administration for their lip-service to the Latin-American republics that did nothing to actually aid them in their fight for independence.[lxxiv] Adams remained unrepentant, stating, "Wherever the standard of freedom and independence has been or shall be unfurled, there will her (America's) heart, her benedictions, and her prayers be. But she goes not abroad in search of monsters to destroy."[lxxv]

Designing America's foreign policy with the Great Powers of Europe, the new republics of the New World, and the future as well, Adams could say with some justification, "Of the public history of Mr. Monroe's administration all that will be worth telling to posterity hitherto has been transacted through the Department of State."[lxxvi] Adams served as the voice and pen of the Monroe administration's foreign policy, but the force of it was backed up by the actions of Jackson. Jackson did what he believed best for the nation with little regard for the whims of his superiors as long as he had the people's support, specifically the white yeomen farmers forming the bulk of the nation's population. Adams, the quintessential Yankee, was born and bred for politics with a legacy of political greatness behind him and a string of successes alongside him, the shadows of both dogging his steps as he worked for the interests of the nation, not its people.

In 1820, the lone electoral vote not to go to Monroe came from New Hampshire, where a single elector, disapproving of Monroe's politics, cast his vote for Adams, who obviously was not running.[lxxvii] But it was clear 1824 would be a very open race. The 1824 presidential election brought all the previously mentioned issues to a head, in a race of political ambitions and regional interests that saw five men step onto the stage of the grandest and to many at the time, the most eyebrow raising election of the young nation.

William H. Crawford of Georgia, the big, jovial Secretary of the Treasury, toed the party line in the past and set his political ambitions aside for the benefit of the Republican establishment, weak as it was. The Party regulars and Crawford himself believed 1824 was his due.[lxxviii] Unfortunately for Crawford and his supporters, he had little appeal beyond the Southern interests, thanks to his proslavery efforts and and the loyal party machine in New York.[lxxix]

**Crawford**

Secretary of State Calhoun of South Carolina also stepped up to the plate, as he would for several elections to come. Ambitious and more cosmopolitan than Crawford, Calhoun's appeal stretched beyond the regional loyalties of the South and the political machines of the Northeast.[lxxx]

Speaker of the House Clay also threw his hat into the ring. Declaring himself the candidate of the West, the charismatic Clay anticipated the saturated race getting thrown into the House of Representatives, where he would have the advantage over his opponents.[lxxxi]

The final two candidates were, unsurprisingly, Adams and Jackson, who offered stark contrasts to the other three. Seeming aloof and moralistic, Adams looked and acted the poster candidate for the Northeast and its Republican interests.[lxxxii] Further, the position of Secretary of State was considered by many at the time as the cabinet position of succession to the presidency.[lxxxiii] Jackson, the senator from Tennessee since 1823, lacked the political connections of his competitors and in fact detested such machinations. A man of the people, Jackson's support lay with the young men serving in state militias who, by the election of 1824, could vote. Given that he was a soldier, the other candidates, with their political machines and connections, did not initially take Jackson's candidacy seriously.[lxxxiv]

Jackson's presidential ambitions went as far back as 1821, when he confided to a friend that he was "at liberty to say in my name both to my friends and enemies – that I will as far as my influence extends Mr. Adams unless Mr. Calhoun should be brought forward."[lxxxv] The election of 1824, as it turned out, included two of Jackson's enemies, and Jackson never forgave his enemies. Besides Calhoun's lambasting of Jackson's actions, Crawford had made the list when he opposed Jackson's efforts against the Creek natives, and he underlined his status on the list when he supported Clay in his efforts against Jackson's conquest of Florida.[lxxxvi]

Adams' succession to the presidency was obviously by no means assured. While the last three presidents came from the same cabinet post he did, those three men were also Virginians. The South held great political sway over the young nation, countering the interests of the Northeast in almost every way, from tariffs to internal improvements and, of course, slavery.[lxxxvii] Adding to his troubles, Adams, aloof and according to some detractors, timid, and a Yankee, faced the imposing figures of Crawford's joviality, Clay's charisma, Calhoun's energy, and Jackson's determination.[lxxxviii]

With regional interests defining the candidates in place of party name, Monroe feared the end of the Era of Good Feelings and the dawn of political parties, something he dreaded with the same vehemence as George Washington.[lxxxix] Into this political maelstrom entered an influential politician who would shape the election: Martin Van Buren, New York Senator and opponent of another upcoming influential politician from the same state, DeWitt Clinton.[xc] With the political machine in New York well-oiled and destined to remain a fixture of state and national politics for generations to come, Van Buren believed he could apply such machinations on the national level as well.[xci] The regional squabbling of the election left him disillusioned and convinced the time was ripe for the birth of a new party – a democratic one.[xcii] Allying with Jefferson and other Old Republicans who believed the lack of parties signified only that the political divisions lacked proper unity, Van Buren prepared to throw his support behind the only candidate he believed aligned with his interests: Crawford.[xciii]

**Van Buren**

While Van Buren prepared to support Crawford, Jackson's friends in Tennessee readied the opposition. With clandestine support from Clay, in 1822 the Tennessee legislature nominated Jackson for the presidency to unanimous approval.[xciv] The legislature stated in their nomination, "The welfare of the country may be safely entrusted [in] the hands of him who has experienced every privation, and encouraged every danger, to promote its safety, its honor, and its glory."[xcv]

Jackson, in the vein of the political gentlemen of the time, refused to politic for the presidential nomination, and was reluctant to accept it. Believing such things were up to the people and not the political machines, Jackson accepted the nomination and quietly refrained from supporting any other candidates.[xcvi] Adams echoed Jackson's political gentlemanliness: "If the presidency was a prize "of cabal and intrigue… I had no ticket in that lottery."[xcvii]

The nominations of 1824, like the Electoral College, changed with the new election. The time of small groups of men, of state legislatures, and congressional caucuses oiling the machines of national politics gave way to a public caucus and an Electoral College decided by popular vote.[xcviii] Though many people condemned the congressional caucuses as the work of intrigue and backroom politics, their supporters still remained, mostly among the political machines of the Northeast and the plantation aristocracy of the South.[xcix] Crawford's support hinged on the old caucus methods, and so his supporters went to work preventing the newest bout of democratization striking the young republic. Clay's supporters also went to work, traveling as far as Louisiana to talk up the so-claimed candidate of the West. Jefferson and Adams, meanwhile, maintained their aloof status, which seemed to not be working as well as it had in the past. Adams especially suffered, as his home turf of New England was reluctant to openly support him until the situation unfolded more clearly.[c]

Though initially Jackson's aloof strategy seemed the same as Adams, it did not take long for the popular hero of New Orleans to gain support. Across the nation, people suspicious of the backroom politicians, who even then struggled to maintain their power so their men could get elected, rallied to the flag of the man who made it quite plain he cared little for political intrigue and even less for its perpetrators.[ci] Jackson's support reached Pennsylvania, the second most populous state at the time. With the ringing endorsement of the *Columbian Observer,* edited by a militia soldier from the Battle of New Orleans, Clay's supporters in Tennessee quickly rallied to Jackson's camp.[cii] Originally put forth to combat Crawford and his supporters, Jackson now found himself a legitimate candidate.

Though Adams did not publicly seek support, he did work behind the scenes to thin the playing field. Recognizing his inability to shine against some of the more charismatic and eloquent candidates, Adams attempted to convince them to seek positions abroad as ambassadors. None of them took the bait, and it was not long before the other candidates started working to sink Adams' ambitions and claim the New England votes for themselves, or at least to make sure Adams did not get them.[ciii] Clay struck at Adams for the Treaty of Ghent, presenting papers that appeared to favor New England fishing interests over the West's very existence. Adams struck back, writing a lengthy pamphlet proving the documents as forgeries.[civ] Jackson lauded Adams' efforts, remarking to his nephew that the pamphlet "has done Mr. Adams much credit, and instead of destroying his popularity in the south and west has increased it."[cv]

Crawford's supporters struck next, accusing Adams of, among other things, being a monarchist. Adams struck back with another pamphlet, proving once again that what skill he lacked with a sword or oration, he more than made up for with his words.[cvi] Some, including Adams' wife, believed he was overdoing it with his poison pen. Worse yet, Adams' defensive writings brought up memories of his father and Adams' own Federalist past.[cvii]

Jackson and Adams grew weary of the competition even in the early stages of the election. Pennsylvania, once thought safely in Calhoun's camp, turned towards Jackson thanks to the controversy regarding the Second Bank of the United States.[cviii] Father Time also took its toll on the nominees, for Crawford's health started failing him. The Georgian suffered a stroke, and his recovery seemed likely but not definitive. In desperation, Van Buren called for a congressional caucus. The other candidates urged a boycott, and the caucus, held on February 14, 1824, had nearly 200 absent members.[cix] It took all of Van Buren's political skills to keep Crawford in the race, for he saw things through a party machine lens; to him, Crawford was the Republican candidate, and that meant he was the next president.[cx]

The political dealings of the caucus and its aftermath sickened Jackson, but even so it became clear the field needed thinning somehow. Supporters of each camp looked to bridge regions for greater support, even as regional rivalries made themselves plain. Crawford and Calhoun and Jackson and Clay could clearly benefit from uniting their regional interests, except for the fact that neither pair could stand their opposite.[cxi]

Adams, the odd man out, actually benefited from this, because whoever he worked with, whether for a running mate or simply to undermine the opposition, Adams could choose South or West without coming to blows with his own regional support as long as he played his cards right. With his own support going to Jackson, Calhoun started testing the waters for the vice presidency, both for himself and Jackson, who Adams considered for the vice presidency himself.[cxii] Adams put out feelers for Jackson as vice president, going so far as to host a social event at his house on January 8, the anniversary of the Battle of New Orleans. Jackson, of course, accepted.[cxiii]

Despite attending the party and the cordial relations between Jackson and Adams, Jackson remained aloof throughout the election, though he continued to rail against Crawford, stating to a friend that his choice as president "would be a great curse to the nation."[cxiv] He also found himself forced to take stances on the controversial issues of the time despite his efforts to maintain a distant, traditional election.[cxv]

Still, Jackson did enjoy the attention, as the tall, frontier general stuck out quite a bit from the normal politicians. For people used to the cantankerous soldier who executed two foreign nationals with a farce of a trial, his meeker, more nuanced behavior raised a few impressed eyebrows.[cxvi]

While Jackson remained reluctant to state his positions on controversial issues in public, he had no shortage of trusted friends to confide in, serving as a much needed venting system for a man who normally made his opinions very plain, and very loudly. One issue that earned his ire was federal funding for internal improvements; while Crawford and his supporters lauded such action, Jackson opposed it, fearing that any increase in federal power would "produce in the end a consolidation of the States, to the utter destruction of those checks and balances…at present existing under our confederation."[cxvii]

Protective tariffs proved another issue Jackson could not keep completely silent on, and the decisive issue came to the forefront of the election, especially with a new tariff up for vote prior to the election. Clay, representing the farming interests in his home state and the West in general, supported the tariffs as the best way to avoid foreign imports.[cxviii] As a Westerner with Southern support, both regions supporting the tariffs, Jackson treaded carefully to avoid alienating his tepid Northeastern support, supporting a modest tariff in 1824 that he managed to tie to both the old standbys of supporting American farmers and industry, and his Anglophobia.[cxix]

With five hats in the ring, it was only a matter of time before regionalism and factionalism took their toll on the ostensibly one party race. Calhoun withdrew first. With Jackson's superior popularity apparent, and consoling himself that for a politician he was still fairly young at 42, he declared his willingness to settle for the vice presidency. In those times the Electoral College decided such things, and the vote went overwhelmingly to Calhoun.[cxx]

Despite Calhoun's support, many continued to talk of an Adams-Jackson or Jackson-Adams ticket. Both men refrained from committing to such a ticket for their own reasons. Adams, naturally withdrawn, preferred to mull such things over himself, bearing the weight of his political legacy as best he could.[cxxi] Jackson, in contrast, maintained that he had little interest in the election as long as his enemies were not elected.[cxxii]

With the election approaching and one name out of the running, the stage was set for a grand political show that would set the stage for 1828. No parties were vying for votes and support, so regionalism ruled the day, even if each candidate had their supporters across the nation. As regional interests threatened to take over, the press stressed the need for a pan-regional government, lest the interests of one section dominate politics.[cxxiii] Several newspapers extolled Jackson for this, stating a candidate of the West was best suited to represent the nation at large, thanks to the West's distance from the Southern and Northern interests, and the need for rural people to band together regardless of class. The West then was the seat of democratization in the young nation.[cxxiv] Alongside their support of the West, several Southern papers railed against New England and their attacks on southern ways, mainly slavery.[cxxv]

The press having said their piece and the politician's supporters theirs, the time for the election finally arrived. Despite the efforts of the party machine to have their man elected – even as that man lay recovering from a debilitating stroke – 18 of the young nation's 24 states now used popular votes to direct the Electoral College.[cxxvi] Since communication and transportation infrastructure were still developing, no set voting date existed. As both popular and electoral votes trickled in, Jackson quickly gained a plurality of the electors, seizing 42.5 percent of the popular vote and 99 electors.[cxxvii] Adams received 31.5 percent of the popular vote and 84 electoral votes. Clay and Crawford both received 13 percent of the vote and 37 and 41 electors, respectively.[cxxviii]

Unsurprisingly, Jacksons' greatest support lay in the South and West. Indeed, every Southern state except Georgia went to him. He also won Illinois and Indiana in the West, Pennsylvania, and the states of New Jersey, Delaware, and Maryland, along with a few electoral votes from other states which allowed electoral votes divided by the popular vote's results.[cxxix] Adams received his due of New England, along with a handful of electoral votes from other states based on popular vote divisions. Clay took a chunk of New York's votes, Kentucky, Ohio, and Missouri. Crawford received his home state of Georgia, Virginia, and a handful of New York's electors.[cxxx]

Divided amongst four candidates with no clear winner, the election found itself thrown to the House of Representatives for the first time since 1800. Article Twelve of the Constitution stipulated the top two candidates would be chosen by the House, knocking Clay out of the race and leaving Crawford, thanks to his health and lack of popular support, in the dust. As the race narrowed on Jackson and Adams, each state received one vote, and it did not take long for Adams to begin wheeling and dealing, for the realm of such politics flowed in his blood and he preferred working privately to the more public actions of his new rival.[cxxxi]

Adams was not the only one politicking. As Speaker of the House, Clay still held plenty of power in this part of the election. Though the two were less then amiable in the past due to matters involving negotiations at Ghent to end the War of 1812, the two spoke privately for several hours to reach a mutually beneficial agreement.[cxxxii] Clay, fearful of having an insubordinate warmonger like Jackson as president, threw his support behind Adams, and with Ohio, Kentucky, and Missouri behind him, Adams received enough votes to become President of the United States, much to the joy of his father.[cxxxiii] A burgeoning Jacksonian named John Randolph, from Virginia, remarked to his fellow Jackson supporters, "It was impossible to win the game gentlemen. The cards were stacked."[cxxxiv] A Louisiana man – Louisiana having turned to support Adams in the House - Randolph railed against his state's betrayal for turning against the hero of New Orleans.[cxxxv] Jackson's nephew also complained of the backroom intrigue, "That Mr. Adams should swear to support the constitution of the United States which he purchased from Representatives who betrayed the constitution, and which he must distribute among them as rewards for their iniquity."[cxxxvi] Privately, Jackson grumbled, "[Y]ou see here, the voice of the people of the west have been disregarded, and demagogues barter them as sheep in the shambles, for their own views, and personal aggrandizement."[cxxxvii] Of course, Jackson kept his resentment private, appearing less bitter and incensed in public than he actually was. He even congratulated the new president at a formal event shortly after the House vote. Still, he could not hold back a formal barb, offering his left hand as he congratulated Adams, because "for the right, you see, is devoted to the fair."[cxxxviii] Adams replied courteously, and he wrote in his diary that Jackson was courteous as well.[cxxxix]

All the while, Jackson believed himself betrayed by political intrigue, the very thing he despised in Washington. Worse still, a nominal ally and man he believed above such petty dealings not only took part in such dealings, but did so to undermine Jackson. For the bombastic old soldier, this was nothing less than a personal insult.

As Adams prepared for his inauguration, Jackson now mentally added the name of John Quincy Adams to his list of enemies, and Jackson never forgave his enemies.

## Politics during the Adams Presidency

Adams believed himself the best candidate for the presidency, and, besides, Clay sought him out, not the other way around. Still, the backroom deal left a sour taste in his mouth as well. He considered it necessary, but at the same time the fact he needed to do so in order to win the office showed his weaknesses as a candidate, and thus potential weakness in his administration.

For his efforts, Clay received the post of Secretary of State, and the press had a field day, declaring the election bought and its ends the result of a corrupt bargain.[cxl] Already considering Clay an enemy, Jackson said of the new Secretary of State, "The Judas of the West has closed the contract and will receive his thirty pieces of silver. His end will be the same."[cxli]

Jackson had not run for president to become president - he ran to prevent two people he despised becoming president, and in that, at least, he succeeded. Still, retiring to his home after voting against Clay's appointment to Secretary of State, he continued to seethe against the so-called corrupt bargain that denied him the highest office in the young nation.[cxlii] Feeling betrayed by his former supporter, Jackson responded to the Tennessee legislature's nomination for president in 1828 by resigning his Senate seat. Now free from official politics, Jackson could remain politically active with his supporters without having to officially state his opinion on the issues of the day through votes, votes that could come back to haunt him should he choose to run in 1828.[cxliii]

Adams, meanwhile, raised eyebrows with his inaugural address by advocating internal improvements and other controversial expansions of federal power at the time, something that, combined with Clay's appointment as Secretary of State, guaranteed Jackson's supporters would not sit idle for the next four years.[cxliv] Adams' views reflected the oligarchic paternalism of a New England politician, while Jackson trusted the will of the people, if for no other reason than they supported and vindicated his actions when the likes of Adams' supporters (if not Adams himself) criticized them.[cxlv]

Though Adams strived to maintain his predecessor's avoidance of parties and factions, his very ascendance to the presidency created a rift in the last standing party. Observing that rift with the ambitious eye of a man longing for the seat above him, Calhoun, increasingly disenchanted with the president and his decisions, wrote to Jackson in 1826. His letter would crystallize not only the main issues of the day, but also the defining planks of the future partisan divisions.[cxlvi] Calhoun wrote to Jackson that "it must be determined in the next three years, whether the real governing principle in our political system be the power and patronage of the Executive, or the voice of the people.... For it can scarcely be doubted, that a scheme has been formed to perpetuate power in the present hands, in spite of the free and unbiased sentiment of the country."[cxlvii] Jackson spent a month mulling over the letter, hand delivered by a senator, before replying to the ambitious vice president. Once again condemning Adams for his betrayal, Jackson wrote to Calhoun, "I trust my name will always be found on the side of the people, and as their confidence in your talents and virtue has placed you in the second office of government, that we shall march hand in hand together in their cause."[cxlviii]

Thus started a great political alliance, and though it would take more than even two such men as Calhoun and Jackson to change the political arena, it certainly boded an excellent start. All Jackson needed now to avenge his betrayal was a cast of dedicated supporters also smarting under the dangers of increased federal power. In his search would arise an unlikely ally in Van Buren, the Little Magician whose political skills and acumen with machine politics before the machine existed would have made Tammany Hall proud. Originally, to bolster party politics, Van Buren looked not to himself to aid the Jackson movement, but his former candidate Crawford, slowly recovering from his stroke and still on Jackson's list of despised individuals. Worse, Crawford's popularity, shaky as it was to begin with, now appeared reduced to his home state, and Jackson or Calhoun could easily sway Georgia to their side on their own.[cxlix]

Van Buren had his work cut out for him in the 1828 election, but such were the sort of games the Little Magician loved. With their eyes on the presidential election of 1828, the midterm elections of 1826 witnessed an energy unseen in previous midterms. Van Buren went to work rallying Jackson's supporters; he sent a letter to supporters in Virginia while making sure the likes of Calhoun saw the letter as well.[cl] Convinced of the need of a party machine and wary of bipartisanship, Van Buren wrote, "We must always have party distinctions, and the old ones are the best of which the nature of the case admits. Political combinations between the inhabitants of the different states are unavoidable & the most natural & beneficial to the country is that between the planters of the South and the plain republicans of the north."[cli]

As 1826 turned to 1827, the Jacksonians prepared for the coming election. While Adams' administration floundered against anti-federal resistance, Van Buren toured the South to rally Jackson's supporters and bring a new era to American politics. Aware that Van Buren acted effectively as Jackson's campaign manager, Adams kept a close eye on the Little Magician.[clii] Those who supported Adams and opposed Jackson were at the time called The Anti-Jacksonian Party (the term "National Republican Party" did not come about until after the election).[cliii] Opposing Adams and his federalism, Jackson and his group hailed from the Democratic-Republican Party of Thomas Jefferson, the party that still remained during the Era of Good Feelings. Resurrecting the name to set them apart from the National Republicans, Jackson's party would not be called the Democratic Party until after the election.[cliv]

From the lone party standing after the War of 1812 rose two new parties, and these truly were parties, with machine politics, media blitzes, and campaigning the likes of which the United States had never seen before. The first modern election dawned on the young nation, and it would prove an especially nasty and personal campaign, one that still ranks among the dirtiest in history.

## The Rematch

The election of 1828 was the first in which candidates appealed directly to the people for votes. While it was the first election where this could be done fully and properly, the early efforts of Jackson's supporters in 1824 laid the groundwork for the efforts in 1828. Ethnic voting blocs, media campaigns, polling, rallies, and fundraising were all used by the Jacksonians to fight back against the future National Republicans, taking the campaign to the people instead of the politicians.[clv]

Another important ally for the Democratic-Republicans was the press. Several prominent newspapers in Virginia, Washington, and New York supported Jackson, bringing the weight of the Fifth Estate to bear against Adams and his policies. Not only did these newspapers support Jackson, but thanks to their spread and increase in number, the press could coordinate and network across the nation as never before, allowing them to cast a wide net of media saturation unseen in previous elections.[clvi] With the nation as their audience and Washington their stage, the two burgeoning parties prepared for the greatest show the nation would yet witness.

It did not take long for the mud to start slinging and for things to get personal. Inevitably, Jackson proved an easy target, thanks to his past record of insubordination and rough frontier appearance and style, but the fact that his constituents liked all that about him prevented Adams' supporters from striking back with full effect.

However, even as Jackson seemed immune to such personal attacks, his wife was another matter.[clvii] Jackson and Rachel's marriage remained a scandal in both their lives, as the woman's divorce prior to Jackson's marriage was not entirely complete when the two married. The pro-Adams press, in the stuffy vein of New England Yankeeism, struck hard against Rachel, with one paper remarking, "Anyone approving of Andrew Jackson must therefore declare in favor of the philosophy that any man wanting anyone else's pretty wife has nothing to do but take his pistol in one hand a horsewhip in another and possess her."[clviii]

**Rachel Jackson**

Jackson struggled to protect his wife, whom he loved dearly, from the attacks, and the incessant assaults by the press worsened her already ill health. At one point, she allegedly confided to a friend that she "would rather be a doorkeeper in the house of God than live in that palace in Washington." She would die in December, likely from a heart attack, shortly before Jackson was supposed to leave for Washington. True to form, he never forgave those who he blamed for worsening his wife's depression and ultimately killing her. At her funeral, he remarked, "May God Almighty forgive her murderers. I never can."[clix]

The press also attacked Jackson's mother, a move that drove Old Hickory to tears. Utilizing all capitals and far too many exclamation points, one paper called her "a common prostitute, brought to this country by British soldiers. She afterward married a MULATTO MAN, with whom she had several children, of which number General JACKSON is one!!!"[clx]

The most effective attacks by the pro-Adams press consisted of insinuations that during the Creek War of 1813, Jackson murdered several of his militiamen, for no better reason than his lust for violence. Accompanied by a graphic image of six named coffins, the article, titled "Some

Account of Some of the Bloody Deeds of General Jackson," portrayed Jackson as a bloody-minded maniac who fought and killed for the sheer joy of it.[clxi]

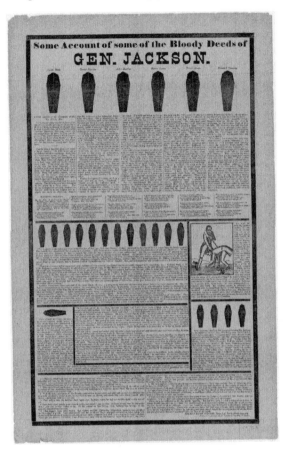

**The political ad**

This time, the Jacksonian press struck back, retorting that the six militiamen were not murdered but executed for mutiny following a fair trial. This also had the added benefit of suggesting that when it came to his own countrymen, Jackson could follow the law if he needed to.[clxii]

Having fought back with facts, the pro-Jackson press felt no compunction about taking an eye for an eye in the game of mudslinging. Though Adams proved willing enough to shoot his own campaign in the foot, it was the so-called corrupt bargain of 1824 that continued to draw the Jacksonians' ire.[clxiii]

Moreover, the Jacksonian press attacked Adams' religion, accusing him both of being anti-Christian for quoting Voltaire at a toast one evening, and for his Puritan roots. They also accused him of offering a young American girl to Czar Alexander I. At the root of the smear campaign was that Adams' federalism reeked of monarchism, and that "his habits and principles are not congenial with the spirit of our institutions and notions of a democratic people."[clxiv]

The enlarged presence of media usage was thanks to the press network mentioned earlier. Calhoun and Crawford supporters, aligned with the Jackson camp thanks to the efforts of Calhoun and Van Buren, did the work of the party press.[clxv] A Virginia paper under a former Crawford supporter named Thomas Ritchie set out the planks of the Jackson campaign as set forth by Van Buren. Struggling to prevent the sectionalism of North and South, Van Buren urged Ritchie to rally the southern radicals behind them to form a new party with similar minded individuals in the north.[clxvi]

**Ritchie**

Despite this, the parties quickly took up regional lines, with the Nationals claiming the northeast while Jackson claimed the south and west. The Jackson camp's media surge not only outweighed the National Republicans, the Jackson leaders themselves coordinated far more thoroughly than their National rivals, meeting regularly during Congressional sessions to plan and coordinate their efforts.[clxvii] Thanks to these leaders coming from all corners of the nation, combined with the vast network of local and regional papers swayed to their side, the sheer weight of the Jackson campaign struck hard and fast against the Nationals.

Media awareness was all well and good, but with the transition to a popular vote over state legislatures choosing electors, the Jacksonians faced the unique task of making sure their constituents actually voted.[clxviii] To do this, the Jackson camp sponsored and started various clubs and committees throughout the nation, planting hickory trees and rallying crowds as campaigners spoke out in praise of Jackson's ticket and condemnation of the current administration. In the south, Jackson's supporters merely arrived at militia musters or other such events to speak and rally the people in support of Old Hickory.[clxix]

The Adams' campaign tried to match the Jacksonians' efforts, but they lacked the energy of their opponents, failing to rally the people and drum up the type of crowds and enthusiasm the Jackson camp raised with their efforts. Compounding the problem was the lack of coordination of the National Republicans - most of the work fell on Clay's shoulders, but he spent most of his efforts defending himself against the "corrupt bargain" accusations continually trumpeted by the press.[clxx] Worse still, Adams lacked regional support beyond the Northeast, and he could never effectively campaign in the South, West, or the new Northern states west of Pennsylvania.[clxxi]

Of course, committees, clubs, and newspapers required funding, and the 1828 campaign witnessed new heights when it came to fundraising and financial expenditures for presidential elections. Banks in New York and Pennsylvania provided a great deal of funding for the Jackson campaign at Van Buren's urging, but the bulk of the finances came from the committees and rallies themselves, where dues, printing costs and even public dinners with a cost of five dollars swelled the Jacksonian treasury.[clxxii]

Jackson himself also entered the fray, campaigning as no presidential candidate had before, shaking hands and burying hatchets to consolidate power and gather votes while staying carefully quiet about decisive issues like the tariff.[clxxiii] Having only served as a Senator for a short time, even his limited political history at the national level was advantageous, as it protected him from contentious issues, at least aside from the issues of slavery and Indian removal, where Jackson's military and civilian history spoke loud and clear on such matters.[clxxiv]

Adams, in contrast, struggled to remain personally above the political squabble, appearing as aloof and disinterested as he did in 1824. Unfortunately for him, that aloofness and aversion to factionalism now ran counter to the people's will, and in the election of 1828, the people's will translated to votes in a way the National Republicans never fully grasped.[clxxv] The call to the people and not the politicians culminated for the Jacksonians during the 13th anniversary of the Battle of New Orleans. Their coordination allowed them to organize celebrations across the nation, capped off with a visit to New Orleans by Jackson himself.[clxxvi] Although the event had its critics (Adams griped in his diary that Jackson's speech seemed written by someone else even though it was not), Jackson's visit received widespread news coverage, marking it as the first true presidential media event in the young country's history.[clxxvii]

Facing overwhelming odds, Adams' camp trudged on, fighting back against the burgeoning Democratic onslaught as best it could. An accusation that the president purchased a billiard table with public funds roused the Adams camp, which maintained it was purchased with personal money, but with no major leaders to organize defense or offense, the accusation just added to the weight stacked against the National Republicans.[clxxviii]

All the while, even as Jackson felt no compunction about campaigning, Adams still refused such efforts, declining to attend events that could easily work to his campaign's advantage and rouse support for the cause. Not particularly fond of crowds, the aloof style of political maneuvering that won him the presidency in 1824 now worked against him as the people's voice thundered above the din of political wheeling and dealing.[clxxix] Rather than campaign for the election or even support others in their campaigns, Adams withdrew into his work and legal studies, creating a protective personal shell as the Jacksonian machine steamed ahead into a new era of politics.[clxxx]

Still, Adams could look back on his administrative efforts with some success. Though the Jacksonians stymied many of his efforts, the Adams administration had done a fair job on the whole. Under Adams, foreign trade and relations improved and increased, and the Creeks of Georgia, now mostly settled farmers, received a reprieve from the long dreaded removal west. That reprieve would end after Jackson won the coming election.[clxxxi]

Had the Adams campaign been better coordinated, better led, and more widespread, it could have reached out to the Western vote, where the desire for internal improvements and increased federal support resonated loudest outside New England. The National Republicans tried to strike against the Jacksonians with a new protective tariff, but the effort lacked Adams' official support and failed to separate the Northern Democrats from their Southern brethren, though they did manage to pass the tariff.[clxxxii]

The Adams' campaign also tried to strike back in other ways, utilizing opposition research for the first time to dig up dirt on Jackson, which was hardly a difficult task. The biggest problem for Adams' detractors was that everything about Jackson led in some way or another to the Battle of New Orleans, and that legacy resonated so strongly with the voter base that it overshadowed any negative smudges on Jackson's past.[clxxxiii]

As the election neared and party tickets once again became a part of American politics, Calhoun jumped ship to join with Jackson. Adams selected as his vice presidential candidate Richard Rush, his Secretary of the Treasury, meaning that for the first time in American history, two Northerners ran against two Southerners. This was a slap to Van Buren's efforts to avoid sectionalism but a boon to his efforts to protect slavery.[clxxxiv] Another issue as the election neared was the matter of electors, as the manner of their selection and the elections surrounding them and other national seats still lacked proper coordination and organization on the national level.[clxxxv]

**Rush**

The Jacksonians, unsurprisingly, reached out as never before to get out the word to vote, unleashing a flurry of pamphlets in multiples languages to make sure the nation's already multi-ethnic population went to the polls on the required day. Pamphlets in German, French, and English spread across the nation, urging people, "The faithful sentinel must not sleep –Let no one stay home. –Let every man go to the polls –Let not a vote be lost –Let each Freeman do his duty; and all will triumph in the success of JACKSON, CALHOUN, and LIBERTY."[clxxxvi] The Nationals sedately called on its supporters, "Let no man stay home; but let each set an example worthy of the emulation of his neighbors: let the young and healthy assist the aged and sick in reaching the polls."[clxxxvii]

In the end, the Democratic-Republicans received 178 electoral votes, 56 percent of the popular vote, and carried every state outside of New England and the Mid-Atlantic border states, as well as four of New York's 20 delegates and one of Maine's nine.[clxxxviii] The National Republicans received 83 electoral votes, roughly 43.6% of the popular vote, and the federal stronghold of New England, as well as the votes previously mentioned.[clxxxix] Jackson won the day, and this time there would be nothing the House of Representatives could do about it.

Adams was the first incumbent president not re-elected, and the reasons ring clear amidst the onslaught of the Jackson campaign. For the first time in presidential history, the two factions rallied their supporters as never before, and in many ways, it was the Democratic-Republicans who pioneered such efforts. They utilized fundraisers, rallies, and clubs to get the word out to vote in support of their platform, and they denounced their opposition with incendiary language and slander, thereby successfully smearing their opponent and extolling their own cause simultaneously.

The National Republicans fought back with opposition research and rallies of their own, but they failed to capture the energy and zeal of their opponents. As Adams despondently looked ahead to the end of his only term, a new era dawned in American politics, and the two-party system returned to the young nation. Though the parties would themselves change over time, the election of 1828 resonates as the first true modern election, the harbinger of a system that still exists today.

**Online Resources**

Other books about 19th century American history by Charles River Editors

Other books about the Election of 1828 on Amazon

**Bibliography**

Brinkley, Alan and Davis Dyer. The American Presidency: The Authoritative Reference. Boston: Houghton Mifflin Company, 2004.

Hecht, Marie B. *John Quincy Adams: A Personal History of an Independent Man (Signature Ser.))* (1995)

Hubbard, Elbert and Fra Elbert. *John Quincy Adams* (2010)

Lewis, James E. *John Quincy Adams: Policymaker for the Union (Biographies in American Foreign Policy)* (2001)

Meacham, Jon. American Lion: Andrew Jackson in the White House. New York: Random House, 2008.

Morse, John T. *John Quincy Adams* (2008)

Morse, John T. Jr. *John Quincy Adams: American Statesmen Series* (2007)

Nagel, Paul C. *John Quincy Adams: A Public Life, a Private Life* (1999)

Parsons, Lynn. *John Quincy Adams (American Profiles)* (1999)

Philips, Douglas. *The Bible Lessons of John Quincy Adams for His Son (Profiles in Fatherhood)* (2001)

Quincy, Josiah. *Memoir of the life of John Quincy Adams.* (2012)

Remini, Robert V. and Arthur M. Schlesinger. *John Quincy Adams (The American Presidents Series)* (2002)

Remini, Robert V. Andrew Jackson and the Course of American Empire, 1767-1821. New York: Harper Row, 1977.

Richards, Leonard. *The Life and Times of Congressman John Quincy Adams* (1988)

Seward, William H. *Life and Public Services of John Quincy Adams Sixth President of the Unied States* (2011)

Smith, Carter and Allen Weinstein. Presidents: Every Question Answered. New York: Hylas Publishing, 2004.

Unger, Harlow G. *John Quincy Adams* (2012)

Weeks, William E. *John Quincy Adams and American Global Empire* (2002)

Wheelan, Joseph. *Mr. Adams's Last Crusade: John Quincy Adams's Extraordinary Post-Presidential Life in Congress* (2009)

## Free Books by Charles River Editors

We have brand new titles available for free most days of the week. To see which of our titles are currently free, click on this link.

## Discounted Books by Charles River Editors

We have titles at a discount price of just 99 cents everyday. To see which of our titles are currently 99 cents, click on this link.

---

[i] Parsons, Lynn H., *The Birth of Modern Politics: Andrew Jackson, John Quincy Adams, and the Election of 1828* (2009), pg. 3-5.

[ii] Ibid, 6-7.

[iii] Ibid, 7.

[iv] Ibid, 7.

[v] Ibid, 7.

[vi] Ibid, 7.

[vii] Ibid, 7.

[viii] Ibid, 8-9.

[ix] Ibid, 9.

[x] Ibid, 10-11.

[xi] Ibid, 3.

[xii] Ibid, 11.

[xiii] Ibid, 11, New England being the largest commercial base in the young nation at the time. That the Republican Party at this time included the Southern plantation owners, representing the southern oligarchy, is naturally hilariously ironic.

[xiv] Ibid, 13. oops

[xv] Ibid, 16-17.

[xvi] Ibid, 20-21.

[xvii] Ibid, 21.

[xviii] Ibid, 21.

[xix] Howe, Daniel W., *What Hath God Wrought: the transformation of America, 1815-1848.* New York: Oxford University Press (2007), pg. 743.

[xx] Parsons, *The Birth of Modern Politics*, pg. 32-33. Also ironic for it occurring after the war ended, communication being somewhat slow at the time.

[xxi] "Electoral College Box Scores 1789-1996", National Archives and Records Administration, retrieved January 6, 2018.

[xxii] Ibid. Delaware's status as a minor port hub at the time making it effectively a New England state in terms of regional interests at the time.

[xxiii] Howe, *What Hath God Wrought*, pg. 92.

[xxiv] Parsons, *The Birth of Modern Politics*, pg. 37.

[xxv] Ibid, 38.

[xxvi] Ibid, 39.

[xxvii] Ibid, 39-40.

[xxviii] Ibid, 42-43.

[xxix] Ibid, 43-44.

[xxx] Ibid, 44-45.

[xxxi] Ibid, 46.

[xxxii] Howe, *What Hath God Wrought*, pg. 98.

[xxxiii] Ibid, 98. Spain allied with the Americans during the Revolution because of familial ties to France. Spain never liked the alliance with the US, and the US never liked the Catholic monarchy, either.

[xxxiv] Ibid, 98.

[xxxv] Ibid, 98.

[xxxvi] Parsons, *The Birth of Modern Politics*, pg. 48.

[xxxvii] Howe, *What Hath God Wrought*, pg. 99-100, Parsons, *The Birth of Modern Politics*, pg. 48-49.

xxxviii Parsons, *The Birth of Modern Politics*, pg. 48-49.

xxxix Howe, *What Hath God Wrought*, pg. 100-102.

xl Quoted in Parsons, *The Birth of Modern Politics*, pg. 52.

xli Quoted in Ibid, 52.

xlii Quoted in Ibid, 52.

xliii Howe, *What Hath God Wrought*, pg. 102-103.

xliv Quoted in Parsons, *The Birth of Modern Politics*, pg. 52-53.

xlv Ibid, 53.

xlvi Quoted in Ibid, 53.

xlvii Ibid, 54-55.

xlviii Quoted in Ibid, 55.

xlix Ibid, 55.

l Howe, *What Hath God Wrought*, pg. 106-107.

li Ibid, 107.

lii Ibid, 107-108.

liii Ibid, 108.

liv Howe, *What Hath God Wrought*, pg. 108.

lv Ibid, 108.

lvi Ibid, 113.

lvii The Adams-Onis Treaty of 1819, Article 3, https://web.archive.org/web/20160923113039/http://www.tamu.edu/faculty/ccbn/dewitt/adamonis.htm, accessed January 9, 2018.

lviii Ibid, 112.

lix Ibid, 111.

lx The Monroe Doctrine, 1823, https://web.archive.org/web/20120108131055/http://eca.state.gov/education/engteaching/pubs/AmLnC/br50.htm, accessed January 10, 2018.

lxi Ibid.

lxii Quoted in Parsons, *The Birth of Modern Politics*, pg. 56.

lxiii Ibid, 56.

lxiv Ibid, 56.

lxv Ibid, 57.

lxvi Ibid, 57-58.

lxvii Ibid, 61-62.

lxviii Ibid, 63.

lxix Ibid, 63.

lxx Ibid, 63.

lxxi Quoted Ibid, 64.

lxxii Quoted in Ibid, 64.

lxxiii Ibid, 64.

lxxiv Ibid, 65.

lxxv Quoted in Ibid, 65. At least not for another couple hundred years.

lxxvi Quoted in Ibid, 66.

lxxvii Ibid, 66.

lxxviii Howe, *What Hath God Wrought*, pg. 203.

lxxix Ibid, 203

lxxx Ibid, 204.

lxxxi Ibid, 204-205.

lxxxii Ibid, 204-205.

lxxxiii Parsons, *The Birth of Modern Politics*, pg. 70.

lxxxiv Howe, *What Hath God Wrought*, pg. 205.

lxxxv Parsons, *The Birth of Modern Politics*, pg. 70.

lxxxvi Ibid, 70.

lxxxvii Ibid, 70.

lxxxviii Ibid, 70-71.

[lxxxix] Ibid, 72.

[xc] Ibid, 72.

[xci] Ibid, 73.

[xcii] Ibid, 73-74.

[xciii] Ibid, 74-75.

[xciv] Ibid, 75, Howe, *What Hath God Wrought*, pg. 206.

[xcv] Parsons, *The Birth of Modern Politics*, pg. 75-76.

[xcvi] Ibid, 76.

[xcvii] Quoted in Ibid, 76.

[xcviii] Howe, *What Hath God Wrought*, pg. 207.

[xcix] Parsons, *The Birth of Modern Politics*, pg. 77-78.

[c] Ibid, 78-79.

[ci] Ibid, 79.

[cii] Ibid, 79-80.

[ciii] Ibid, 80-81.

[civ] Ibid, 81.

[cv] Quoted in Ibid, 81.

[cvi] Ibid, 81.

[cvii] Ibid, 81-82.

[cviii] Ibid, 82.

[cix] Ibid, 83.

[cx] Ibid, 83.

[cxi] Ibid, 83.

[cxii] Howe, *What Hath God Wrought*, pg. 206, Parsons, *The Birth of Modern Politics*, pg. 83.

[cxiii] Parsons, *The Birth of Modern Politics*, pg. 84.

[cxiv] Quoted in Ibid, 84.

[cxv] Ibid, 84.

[cxvi] Ibid, 85.

[cxvii] Ibid, 85.

[cxviii] Ibid, 85-86.

[cxix] Ibid, 86.

[cxx] Howe, *What Hath God Wrought*, pg. 207. Specifically, of the 260 electoral votes and 130 needed for the post, Calhoun received 182, over six times the number of votes as the runner-up, Nathan Stanford.

[cxxi] Parsons, *The Birth of Modern Politics*, pg. 86.

[cxxii] Ibid, 86.

[cxxiii] Ibid, 88.

[cxxiv] Ibid, 88-89.

[cxxv] Ibid, 89.

[cxxvi] Howe, *What Hath God Wrought*, pg. 207.

[cxxvii] Ibid, 208.

[cxxviii] Ibid, 208.

[cxxix] Parsons, *The Birth of Modern Politics*, pg. 98-99.

[cxxx] Ibid, 98-99.

[cxxxi] Ibid, 208-209.

[cxxxii] Ibid, 209.

[cxxxiii] Ibid, 209.

[cxxxiv] Quoted in Parsons, *The Birth of Modern Politics*, pg. 104.

[cxxxv] Ibid, 104-105.

[cxxxvi] Quoted in Ibid, 105.

[cxxxvii] Quoted in Ibid, 104.

[cxxxviii] Quoted in Ibid, 105.

[cxxxix] Ibid, 105.

[cxl] Ibid, 106.

[cxli] Quoted in Ibid, 106.

[cxlii] Ibid, 109.

cxliii Ibid, 110-111.

cxliv Ibid, 111-112.

cxlv Ibid, 114-115.

cxlvi Ibid, 120.

cxlvii Quoted in Ibid, 120-121.

cxlviii Quoted in Ibid, 121-122. Ironically Calhoun would become one of two people Jackson would regret not kill in his later years, the other being Clay.

cxlix Ibid, 125-126.

cl Ibid, 126-127.

cli Quoted in Ibid, 127.

clii Ibid, 130.

cliii Howe, *What Hath God Wrought*, pg. 275.

cliv Ibid, 275.

clv Parsons, *The Birth of Modern Politics*, pg. 133.

clvi Ibid, 134.

clvii Swint, Kerwin C., *Mudslingers: The Top 25 Negative Political Campaigns of All Time, Praeger Publishers, (2006), pg. 215.*

clviii Quoted in Ibid, 216.

clix Ibid, 216.

clx Quoted in Ibid, 216.

clxi Ibid, 216-217.

clxii Ibid, 216.

clxiii Ibid, 219.

clxiv Ibid, 219-220.

clxv Parsons, *The Birth of Modern Politics*, pg. 135.

clxvi Howe, *What Hath God Wrought*, pg. 279-280.

clxvii Parsons, *The Birth of Modern Politics*, pg. 136-137.

clxviii Ibid, 138.

clxix Ibid, 138.

clxx Ibid, 138.

clxxi Ibid, 139.

clxxii Ibid, 140.

clxxiii Ibid, 140-141.

clxxiv Ibid, 141.

clxxv Ibid, 141.

clxxvi Ibid, 147.

clxxvii Ibid, 148.

clxxviii Ibid, 150-151.

clxxix Ibid, 152.

clxxx Ibid, 153.

clxxxi Ibid, 154-155. Adams' support of the Creeks in Georgia would result in his name not appearing on the ballot.

clxxxii Ibid, 156-157.

clxxxiii Ibid, 163.

clxxxiv Ibid, 171.

clxxxv Ibid, 177-178.

clxxxvi Quoted in Ibid, 180.

clxxxvii Quoted in Ibid, 180.

clxxxviii Ibid, 182.

clxxxix Ibid, 182.

87547360R00026

Made in the USA
Lexington, KY
26 April 2018